...With God, all things are possible...

FACING THE GIANTS

BIBLE STUDY

Michael Catt   Stephen Kendrick   Alex Kendrick

AS DEVELOPED WITH
Nic Allen

Published by LifeWay Press® © Copyright 2012 Sherwood Baptist Church
© Copyright 2012 Sherwood Pictures, A Ministry of Sherwood Baptist Church, Albany, GA.

ISBN: 978-1-4158-7547-6
Item: 005533950

Dewey Decimal Classification: 248.84
Subject Heading: FAITH \ CHRISTIAN LIFE \ TRUST

Unless otherwise noted, Scripture quotations are taken from the Holman Christian Standard
Bible®, copyright © 1999, 2000, 2002, 2003 by Holman Bible Publishers. Used by permission.

To order additional copies of this resource:
Write LifeWay Church Resources Customer Service, One LifeWay Plaza; Nashville, TN 37234-0113;
Fax order to 615.251.5933; Phone 1.800.458.2772; E-mail *orderentry@lifeway.com;* Order online
at *www.lifeway.com;* or visit the LifeWay Christian Store serving you.

Printed in the United States of America

Adult Ministry Publishing, LifeWay Christian Resources,
One LifeWay Plaza, Nashville, TN 37234-0152

Contents

About the Authors

Michael Catt is a husband, father of two gr daughters, and senior pastor of Sherwood Ba Church, Albany, Georgia. With Jim McBride, Mic is also executive producer of Sherwood Pictures.

Stephen Kendrick is a husband, father of f and associate pastor of Sherwood Baptist Chu Stephen oversees the church's prayer ministry a produces all Sherwood movies.

Alex Kendrick is a husband, father of six, a associate pastor of Sherwood Baptist Church. He a speaker, actor, writer, and the director of Sherwood movies.

Alex, Stephen, and Michael with Jim McBride (center back), the fourth member of Sherwood Pictures' leadership team.

Nic Allen serves as the Family/Children's Pas at Rolling Hills Community Church in Franl Tennessee. He loves movies because he loves g stories. Nic loves helping people encounter Ch and understand how their stories connect to G bigger narrative.

Nic Allen

About the Movie

Facing the Giants is an action-packed drama about a Christian high school football coach who uses his undying faith to battle the giants of fear and failure.

In six years of coaching, Grant Taylor has never led his Shiloh Eagles to a winning season. After learning that he and his wife Brooke face infertility, Grant discovers that a group of fathers are secretly organizing to have him dismissed as head coach. Devastated by his circumstances, he cries out to God in desperation. When Grant receives a message from an unexpected visitor, he searches for a stronger purpose for his football team.

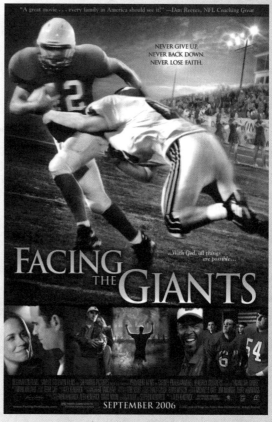

Coach Taylor challenges his players to believe God for the impossible on and off the field. When faced with unbelievable odds, the Eagles must step up to their greatest test of strength and courage. What transpires is a dynamic story of the fight between faith and fear.

www.FacingtheGiants.com • www.LifeWay.com/FacingtheGiants

Facing Your Giants

Head Coach Grant Taylor isn't just facing one giant; he's facing an army of giants. In his own words, he is a failing coach with a failing record. He is facing his own infertility and inability to provide for his wife. In a middle-of-the-night moment of rock-bottom weakness, Grant turns to the Bible and his wife Brooke hits her knees. They realize that turning to God at their weakest moment is perhaps the strongest thing they can do.

The Shiloh Eagles haven't finished with a winning record in six seasons. After revival hits the school and the team, the boys realize that with God all things are possible. For the final game, the boys aren't just facing one giant. They are facing an army of Richland Giants whose sights are set on a fourth consecutive state championship title. The Giants are bigger and stronger than the Shiloh Eagles, but not bigger or stronger than their God!

But this movie isn't about football. It's about faith.

We all face giants. Perhaps you were under the impression at one time that the life of the believer in Jesus Christ was always easy. Perhaps you drew the conclusion at one point that "all things work together for the good of those who love God" (Romans 8:28) means the Christian life should be pain free and void of challenges. But by now you've probably realized just how far from truth those assumptions were. Life happened and you had to make a choice about whether you would trust and love God when it was tough. That's the foundation of this film. That's the essence of faith. That's the purpose of this study.

Your challenges may be similar to the ones highlighted in the film:
- career adversity
- infertility issues
- lack of coworker support
- financial burdens
- losing games

Or perhaps you face a host of different giants:
- market trouble
- marriage woes
- rebellious kids
- massive debt
- sudden death of a loved one
- bleak diagnosis

The list goes on. If you find yourself in Grant Taylor's cleats, you realize that it isn't just one giant you're up against but an army of giants; one new problem piled on top of an already insurmountable lot of difficult life issues. Sometimes, our problems aren't even that big ... on their own. It's when they all come at once that we get overwhelmed.

If this is your story, this Bible study is for you.

If this is not your story, this Bible study is still for you. At one point in life, you'll certainly be stuck under an avalanche of difficult life situations and be in need of stronger faith.

WARNING: The pages in this study are not designed to make your problems go away. They are designed to help you reorient your faith. The steps you take as part of this study are not like medicine, designed to fix an ailment or a symptom. They are more like exercises to stretch, grow, and strengthen your muscles. Muscles grow when resistance or pressure is applied and they learn to respond.

It is time to conquer your fear, face your giants, and grow your faith. Nothing is impossible with God. Whether you win or lose, you must praise Him. Will you? By that measure, your faith is defined. In that manner, your giants are faced ... and they will fall!

How to Use This Study

The *Facing the Giants* 4-week Bible study is organized into sections and can be used for small-group or personal study. Allow 45 to 60 minutes for group sessions.

READ The introductory section of each session contains an illustration to focus your thoughts on the topic of the session. Learners should read the excerpt and be prepared to note and apply transferable principles when prompted by questions in group discussion.

WATCH The Bible Study DVD contains clips from *Facing the Giants* to accompany each of the four sessions. Each clip is 1 to 6 minutes in length and is supported by several discussion questions based on the content of the clip.

DISCUSS This section will be the primary focus of each session. Learners will read Scripture and be prompted to discuss questions related to the Bible passage and study theme for the week. It is most beneficial for each member to prepare with a quick review of the content and Scripture passages prior to the group meeting.

LIVE This section includes a lesson summary and a reflection activity/ challenge to live faithfully in the area of study for each session. Every session includes a Scripture memory challenge and ends with a prayer experience.

Ideally, LIVE is processed as a small group that has experienced all other parts of the session together. This will probably take place most naturally at the beginning of the next week's group session after members have had some time to process the material individually. Yet some activities may be better done privately. However you do it, commit to make meaningful application within your context to conquering your fears, facing your giants, and growing your faith.

Guidelines for Small Groups

The following keys will help to ensure that your group Bible study experience is as meaningful and impactful as possible. *Leader:* Take time during the first meeting to go over all four and ask each participant to commit to the guidelines.

Confidentiality

As you dive into small-group Bible study, group members will be prompted to share thoughts and feelings related to personal struggles they endure. All of these expressions are made out of trust and should be kept with the strictest confidence by the group.

Respect

As trust forms and participants begin to open up about their personal lives, it often becomes easy to offer quick advice. Scripture teaches us to be quick to listen and slow to speak. Listening is the key to respect. Even well meaning advice can be ill received if it isn't requested.

It is important that participants commit to respect one another's thoughts and opinions and to provide a safe place for those thoughts and opinions to be shared without fear of judgment or unsolicited advice.

Preparation

To get the most out of this Bible study, each group member should attend meetings having read through the study and answered questions, ready to discuss the material. Each participant can respect the contribution of the other members by taking the time to be prepared for each session.

Accountability

The goal of the small-group experience is transformation. Each session will help learners identify things about their walk with Christ and their lives that need attention. Each week participants will be asked to commit to take the next step of faith in their lives. As a group, commit together to the account- ability necessary to stay the course and grow your faith.

A Letter to Leaders

Thank you for leading this study. While you will view the movie clips as a group each week, learners should take time to engage the study on their own throughout the week. Encourage participants to spend time reading the Scriptures and responding to prompts so they are prepared to gain the most from the group experience.

Some may ask: why a faith-based film? Or why a Bible study that pulls its illustrations from a movie? It's because of one word: story. Stories are as old as civilization. When you think about it, every legend and fairy tale, novel and film have similar elements. There are characters, settings, and a plot. Within the plot there is an element of conflict and some sort of resolution. There is a purpose, meaning, lesson, or value that can be derived.

Our Lord and Savior Jesus Christ, God in flesh, used stories to communicate valuable truths about Himself and how we are to live in relationship to God. Stories teach us history and tell us truth. They inspire and challenge us. We are motivated and moved by stories. Stories can make us angry and cause us to cry. Stories shape us; they give us a way to tell others who we are.

Movies tell stories with characters, settings, and plots. They make us laugh and cry. They make us angry and motivate us to change ourselves or work harder to change the world around us.

You could easily win an argument about the negative effects of movies today. What was once an undertone of immorality has become the essential element of many top box office hits. In spite of that, you can't argue the power of a popular film. Why wouldn't we celebrate the advent of a faith-based film that not only offers a moral alternative but also tells a great story?

Facing the Giants is your story. It's my story. It's every Christian believer's story at one point or another. Why? Because our faith gets tested. And we can all use one more challenge, one more example, and one more motivation to exercise our faith when faced with life's giants.

Encourage your group to think of the movie as a diving board and God's Word as a swimming pool. The clips you will view help you jump into Scripture and from there swim deep in the wellspring of life, all the while growing your faith. As you facilitate this experience, I encourage you to evaluate your own faith, eliminate your own fears, and battle your own giants. The members in your group will likely only go as deep and be as brave as you are willing to be.

You may be a seasoned leader or this may be your first experience facilitating a group like this. In either case, the following tips will aid your experience:

1. Consider launching your group with a movie-viewing party. Even if members have seen the film already, watching it again as your study begins will familiarize everyone with the characters and key plot elements.

2. Silence can feel deafening in a small-group setting. Far worse, however, is not allowing enough time for people to process and share. Some group members might just need time to process the question or someone's response before taking their turn. Don't be so stressed about silence that you seek to fill every moment with your own sharing. Give people time to think.

3. There is usually at least one person in a group who tends to dominate conversation and at least one who is reluctant to participate. One of your jobs as leader is to help the outgoing member listen more and to elicit participation from the more reserved member. As you guide the discussion, look for ways to inspire a response from the more reserved members but avoid any action that might embarrass them or leave them feeling singled out.

4. Start and end on time. It's not essential to answer every question. If healthy dialogue is taking place, allow that to continue and skip a few questions if necessary. While conversational tangents can steal time, it's typically a lack of preparation by the leader and members that bears the brunt of responsibility. Be prepared each week. Encourage group members to do the same.

As this work is being prepared for print, you are being prayed for. May God bless you and those you minister to through this experience!

WHOLEHEARTED
Apathy vs. Excellence

"I don't care."

"It's not that big a deal."

"God will understand."

"I just don't feel like it right now."

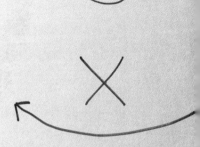

Have you heard these sentiments before? Have you uttered one or more of them yourself? Eleanor Roosevelt said, "So much attention is paid to the aggressive sins, such as violence and cruelty and greed with all their tragic effects, that too little attention is paid to the passive sins, such as apathy and laziness, which in the long run can have a more devastating effect."

Maybe in our culture today it isn't a matter of whether or not we are too hard on some sins but far too light on others. Maybe violence and greed are both too easy a target and apathy is the real culprit to watch. When it comes to a walk with Christ, it is lukewarmness that makes God sick (Revelation 3:16).

The burning question at the center of our faith walk is not whether or not we have any faith at all, but whether we are willing to exercise it wholeheartedly. When it comes to faith, there is no room on God's team for the halfhearted. Apathetic, lazy faith really isn't faith at all. True faith in God requires something from us and inspires something in us. The challenge at hand is to give it our all.

WATCH

MOVIE CLIP

View Clip 1 from the small-group DVD and then use the following discussion to start your study.

SUMMARY

The Eagles are apathetic. They hate losing, but they don't see a way to win. Defensive captain Brock Kelley, the Eagles' most influential leader, expresses a defeatist attitude. Coach Taylor calls Brock out to do a death crawl drill and challenges him to give his absolute best. Blindfolded during the drill, Brock demonstrates wholeheartedness for the first time.

Brock had no idea how far he could go. He was filled with such doubt that he was unwilling to really try. The Eagles were certain that they couldn't win games … so certain in fact that they accepted defeat before the games even began.

OPEN DISCUSSION

1 Have you ever thought that effort was futile? That no matter how hard you tried you couldn't win the game, fix the problem, reach your goal, develop a solution? Describe the situation and your feelings.

Winston Churchill said, "Continuous effort—not strength or intelligence—is the key to unlocking our potential." Coach Taylor knew that. It wasn't about Brock's intelligence, or at least his knowledge of what was going on in that moment. The blindfold took care of that. It wasn't about his strength. He had the ability to carry Jeremy across that field all along. It was about Brock's effort. Before this moment, he didn't believe he could, so he wasn't willing to try.

2 Do you believe you have unlocked all the doors of your own potential? Why or why not? If not, what is holding you back?

3 What is it that you know God desires for you to attempt but you are reluctant to try?

4 In what area of your life have you settled for less than your best? What do you think has made apathy possible in this area?

DISCUSS

Before you can really understand what a book, chapter, or even section of verses means for you today, you have to be willing to examine the historical context. Who wrote it? Why did they write it? When and where did they write it? To whom was the text originally intended? What were the geographical, economic, social, and religious climates like during that day? What does the original language mean? Being able to answer these queries about the text will enhance your knowledge of and appreciation for Scripture and even your own personal application.

Paul wrote Colossians from prison. At the time he had never visited the city in Asia Minor to whom this letter was addressed.

The church was founded by Epaphras, one of Paul's other converts to faith in Christ. In his letter to the church at Colossae, Paul focused on the truth about Christ, which was being battered by false teaching that was infiltrating the church.

In Chapter 3, Paul outlines how we should live our lives in view of Christ. According to Paul, since we are made new in Christ, we must put our focus on Christ and heavenly things (3:1-2); put to death all our fleshly nature and desires (3:5-9); put away unnecessary divisions (3:10-21); put on love and other virtues (3:12-14); and put Christ's peace and His Word into our hearts (3:15-16).

Paul goes on to explain specifically how this Christian nature should infiltrate every area of our status and relationships. Twice in Colossians 3, Paul admonishes believers to do their very best.

COLOSSIANS 3:17,23-24

[17] Whatever you do, in word or in deed, do everything in the name of the Lord Jesus, giving thanks to God the Father through Him. ... [23] Whatever you do, do it enthusiastically, as something done for the Lord and not for men, [24] knowing that you will receive the reward of an inheritance from the Lord. You serve the Lord Christ.

JEREMIAH 29:13-14

[13] "You will seek Me and find Me when you search for Me with all your heart. [14] I will be found by you"—this is the Lord's declaration—"and I will restore your fortunes and gather you from all the nations and places where I banished you"—this is the Lord's declaration. "I will restore you to the place I deported you from."

→ **Read Colossians 3:17,23-24.**

What reasons do these verses give for a value on excellence?

Are there certain things in your life that you do halfheartedly? Explain.

How can you discern whether someone is giving his or her best effort? Describe someone you know who consistently gives his or her best.

According to Colossians 3:17, everything we do should be done in the name of the Lord. As believers, the way we live reflects Christ. Doing our best in all areas reflects Him well. Apathetic, halfhearted living does not. According to verse 23, everything we do should be done as if it is directly for God and not for others. That means we don't complete work assignments to please our boss, coworkers, or even ourselves. We work hard for God. That means we don't exercise to attract others or better ourselves. We exercise to honor God and serve Christ by caring for our bodies.

The essence of these two admonitions from this Colossians 3 passage is that we should do everything with God in mind—school, work, grocery shopping, TV watching, Bible study, family devotion, personal evangelism, exercising, etc.

→ **Read Jeremiah 29:13-14.**

According to this passage, what are the results of seeking God wholeheartedly?

Jeremiah's prophecy is largely gloom and doom. He prophesied about the impending destruction of the people and the subsequent exile to no avail. The people would not listen (Jeremiah 18:12).

In chapter 29 he finally gets to convey a good word from the Lord. God essentially says, "If you come after Me, if you want Me, if you seek Me, you will find Me."

How would you rate yourself when it comes to actively seeking God? Explain your response to the group.

Hard-hearted   Halfhearted   Wholehearted

In what ways do you seek God?

Faith is a gift from God (Ephesians 2:8). But like any gift you receive, it's up to you to use it. That new book won't get read unless you open it. The new TV won't work unless you turn it on. Having enough faith isn't the issue either. It's what you do with the faith you have that matters. Do you use it halfheartedly, just enough to get by? Or do you use it wholeheartedly, with everything you've got?

What factor made the difference in Brock going farther than he thought he could go in the death crawl? He couldn't see. According to 2 Corinthians 5:7, we walk by faith and not by sight.

When we walk (or even crawl) in that faith, wholehearted effort matters.

Memorize Colossians 3:17,23-24 and Jeremiah 29:13-14 this week.

Let these verses script the effort you employ when it comes to everything. Everything you do should be done as if it's representing the name of God and as if it's for God. Give it your all.

GOING DEEPER

As a devotion this week, read John 12:1-8.

One of the most beautiful New Testament pictures of wholehearted love for Jesus was when the woman anointed our Lord at Bethany. A few days before Jesus was crucified, He was visiting the home of Lazarus. Martha served dinner. Mary found a treasured jar of spikenard oil perfume. She broke the jar, poured it on Jesus' feet, and then wiped His feet with her hair.

What is your most prized possession?

How difficult would it be for you to give up that prized possession? If it were a matter of worship, do you think you could give it up?

Why would it be difficult to give it up?
❏ its value   ❏ it was a gift   ❏ it's sentimental
❏ it's part of a collection   ❏ the work or effort it took to get it

The sacrifice that Mary made reflected wholehearted devotion to Jesus. Spikenard was extremely expensive perfume worth about a year's wages (Mark 14:5). Mary could have easily poured just a few drops on Jesus, but she chose to break the jar and use it all. First Corinthians 11:15 tells us that a woman's hair brings her glory. Mary took her most prized possession as well as the thing about her that brought her the most glory and used them both to give Christ worship. Because of Mary's act of worship:

- The entire house was filled with the aroma (John 12:3).
- All of her treasure was spent in honor of Jesus (v. 5).
- Others questioned her sacrifice (v. 4-5).

In Mark 14:9, Jesus said that Mary's story would be told around the world.

Would God consider your worship/sacrifice worth telling others about? Why or why not?

As you look at the temperament of your life, what steps can you take to live more wholeheartedly?

Fulfill Scripture this week by telling someone else the story of John 12:1-8.

PRAYER

Holy God, You are great and mighty. You did not withhold Your precious best when You created this world and offered grace through Your Son to redeem it. Forgive me of my hard-heartedness. Deliver me from those traps and temptations of halfheartedness. Cleanse me of my apathy. Create a faithful heart in me that is wholly devoted to You. May my life be lived in sacrifice. May my worship be fragrant to You. God help me give You my all. Amen.

2

ATTEMPT THE IMPOSSIBLE

FEAR VS. FAITH

In 1983, a 61-year-old potato farmer named Cliff Young attended an annual 543-mile endurance race from Sydney to Melbourne, Australia. This race is considered one of the world's most difficult ultra marathons. Everyone was shocked when they realized that Cliff wasn't there to watch, but to compete. People tried to talk him out of it, but he was ready to run. The press and other athletes were convinced he wouldn't finish. Moreover, they were concerned about his age, his health, and even his running attire. When the race began, the professional runners left the elderly sheepherder in their dust.

Pro athletes knew that in order to complete the race, runners should run 18 hours a day and sleep the remaining 6. They knew it would take approximately 7 days of running those intervals at a good pace. Cliff Young wasn't a pro athlete. The second morning, Australia was stunned to discover that Cliff was not only still in the race, but that he had run all night long. This continued. By the last night, he had passed all of the other runners. He finished the race first, setting a new course record. Now when competing in the Sydney to Melbourne race, runners don't sleep. They run all day and all night just like Cliff Young.

Even more surprising than his victory, Cliff Young was completely unaware that there was a $10k cash prize for the winner. He insisted on giving all of his winnings away to other runners.

There are moments when you catch a glimpse of someone's faith prompting them to dare dreaming beyond what others perceive as possible into the realm of what can only come through the power of God, all for the glory of God.

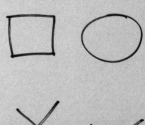

MOVIE CLIP

View Clip 2 from the small-group DVD and then use the following discussion to start your study.

SUMMARY

After trusting God, seeking Him, and honoring Him above themselves, the Shiloh Christian Academy Eagles have won enough football games (and matters of integrity) to earn a spot in the state championship game. Now, as they prepare to face the Giants, the best team in the state, Coach Taylor talks to the team. The Eagles have an impossible task at hand.

OPEN DISCUSSION

1 What are some of the obstacles you have faced in your life? What has been your typical first response (default reaction) to a giant obstacle?

2 Have you or someone you know ever attempted something you thought was impossible? Share the experience.

In this scene Coach Taylor reminds the team about how big, how fast, and how strong the Giants are. Then he tells them to remember how far God has brought them and how hard they have all worked. He points out that they aren't supposed to be here in this moment, but they are.

3. Are you facing anything right now that seems impossible? If so, reflect on how far God has brought you in your thinking about what is possible and what is not. How do you plan to face your obstacle?

DISCUSS

Jesus received word of John the Baptist's death and withdrew (Matthew 14:12-13). Like other moments when the Son of God desired to be alone with God, the crowds followed. They wanted one more moment, one more word, one more taste, and one more miracle from Jesus. The key word is *more*. Skeptics must have thought that Jesus would one day reach a limit where there was nothing more to give. Not so with Jesus. There was always more than enough and He was just about to show them in a really tangible way.

In Matthew 19, Jesus explained to His followers that it would be easier for a camel to go through the eye of a needle than for a rich man to enter heaven (v. 24). This was in response to a rich young ruler who was too dedicated to his life and his things to leave them in order to follow Jesus (vv. 16-22). In response to Jesus' teaching, the disciples recognized the absolute impossibility of being saved. Perhaps before this moment they were still under the impression that what we do (follow the law, follow Jesus) has something to do with salvation.

On one hand, Jesus told them that they were right. With men, salvation is impossible. Take it further: With men, miracles are impossible. With men, giant obstacles are impossible to beat. "With God, all things are possible" (v. 26). People can be healed. Crowds can be fed.

MATTHEW 14:14-21

¹⁴ As He stepped ashore, He saw a huge crowd, felt compassion for them, and healed their sick.

¹⁵ When evening came, the disciples approached Him and said, "This place is a wilderness, and it is already late. Send the crowds away so they can go into the villages and buy food for themselves."

¹⁶ "They don't need to go away," Jesus told them. "You give them something to eat."

¹⁷ "But we only have five loaves and two fish here," they said to Him.

[18] "Bring them here to Me," He said. [19] Then He commanded the crowds to sit down on the grass. He took the five loaves and the two fish, and looking up to heaven, He blessed them. He broke the loaves and gave them to the disciples, and the disciples gave them to the crowds. [20] Everyone ate and was filled. Then they picked up 12 baskets full of leftover pieces! [21] Now those who ate were about 5,000 men, besides women and children.

MATTHEW 19:25-26

[25] When the disciples heard this, they were utterly astonished and asked, "Then who can be saved?"

[26] But Jesus looked at them and said, "With men this is impossible, but with God all things are possible."

Read Matthew 14:14-21.

Describe the circumstances of this event (vv. 14-15).
What were Jesus and His disciples facing in terms of adversity?

Where the disciples only saw the impossible, Jesus made a way.
What does it mean to you to attempt the impossible?

The disciples were certain that the situation was impossible. They reported to Jesus that the time was late and the place desolate. They could only see one solution—send the people away to buy their own food. Jesus saw another option. When we face obstacles, one of the reasons the situation may seem bleak is our tendency to only see one option, usually the most obvious or logical one. What we learn from Scripture is that there is often an alternative. In this case, the alternative was faith.

Do you always believe that God *can* do impossible things? Do you always believe that God *will* do impossible things? Explain.

Why do you think we tend not to live at a greater level of expectancy about the things God can and will do in our lives?

In another movie moment, Coach Taylor has an encounter with Mr. Bridges, an older gentleman who walked the halls of the school praying for students. Mr. Bridges tells Grant a story of two farmers who prayed earnestly for rain. But only one farmer prepared his fields to receive it. There is a difference between believing the impossible and waiting, and believing the impossible and preparing your heart for God to do it.

What do you think it means to prepare for God to do the impossible in your life, in your current situation?

→ Read Matthew 19:25-26.

Is it difficult for you to admit that your situation is impossible for you to handle? Why or why not?

Jesus says, "With men this is impossible, but with God all things are possible." How can we know where we end and God begins?

By definition, *impossible* only means impossible when we try to do things in our own strength.

→ **Memorize Matthew 19:26 and Philippians 4:13 this week.**

> With men this is impossible, but with God all things are possible. **MATTHEW 19:26**

> I am able to do all things through Him who strengthens me. **PHILIPPIANS 4:13**

Write these two verses on note cards and place them in prominent places where you will see them often—the car, the bathroom mirror, your computer screen. As you face various challenges, big and small, remember the importance of trusting God and His strength. *Nothing* is impossible with Him.

GOING DEEPER

For further reflection, read Matthew 14:22-36. All 12 disciples watched as Jesus miraculously healed people and fed 5,000+ with only two fish and five small loaves of bread. But it is possible that only one disciple learned the lesson. Following this miracle, he is the only one we witness attempting to do the impossible in light of his new faith. Peter is often criticized for sinking when he saw the fierce wind and waves, but maybe he should be celebrated for being the only one willing to get out of the boat. The greatest failure isn't sinking. The greatest failure is staying in the boat.

God wants us to be desperate like Peter was when the storm started to rage. As long as we think we can do things in our own strength, we will never be desperate for Him. What does being desperate mean to you?

Many people like to consider the question, "What would you attempt for God if you knew you couldn't fail?" The better question is, "What would you attempt for God in spite of the fact that you may fail?"

PRAYER

Every miracle of God begins with an impossible

situation. We can't meet those moments

with our own might. We need God. Compose

a written prayer in the space below asking

God to increase your faith and to show His

strength in the situation you are facing.

Thank Him for how far He has brought you.

Declare your trust in Him to lead you and

accomplish impossible things through you.

NEVER GIVE UP

DEFEATED VS. DETERMINED

READ

Session 1 began with the phrase, "I don't care." Hopefully you have a new outlook on what it means to strive for excellence in your relationship with God. And hopefully you better understand that excellence in your relationship with Him means giving your best. Today we begin by examining another "I" statement.

"I can't."

Sometimes the "I don't care" statements in life are symptoms of a bigger problem. You don't care about your effort because you don't think you can succeed. Here are some ways that phrase may have reared its ugly head in your life:

"I can't pass, so why even study?"
"I won't get the promotion, so why even apply?"
"We can't afford it, so adoption isn't an option."
"We can't work it out, so marriage counseling would be pointless."

***Can't* is a powerful word.** Some people are motivated by it. If someone tells them they can't do something, they try harder. Some people are tempted by it, desiring everything that seems off limits or out of bounds. Some are crippled by it. They soak it in and allow it to take root in their souls until they believe it. Ultimately, the word *can't* can become a dangerous, self-fulfilling prophecy. We can try to ignore the word but it's better to be inspired by it, to hear it as a reminder of God's ability in our weakness to do the impossible.

In light of our newly restored faith in God's undeniable ability, what we can't do is … give up.

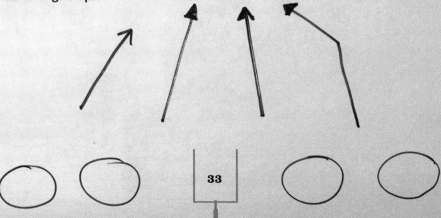

WATCH

MOVIE CLIP

View Clip 3 from the small-group DVD and then use the following discussion to start your study.

SUMMARY

David Childers is small and he's never played football. His background is soccer, but Shiloh doesn't have a soccer team so his dad encourages him to try out for the team's second-string kicker. David misses his first field goal attempt and bemoans his defeat as he talks to his dad after the game. From his wheelchair, David's father challenges his son and his attitude. Because of his own circumstances, David's father seems an unlikely source for words of encouragement, but what he teaches his son in this scene has eternal significance.

OPEN DISCUSSION

1 What do you think caused David to miss the field goal?

In the clip, David's father talks about actions following beliefs. Take the next few minutes to unpack this concept with your group:

2 What is it like to feel "defeated"?

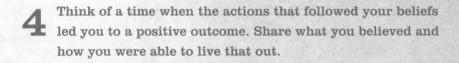

3 How can thinking defeated thoughts lead to living a defeated life?

4 Think of a time when the actions that followed your beliefs led you to a positive outcome. Share what you believed and how you were able to live that out.

The writings of Solomon found in the Book of Proverbs bear the intent of teaching people how to understand and attain wisdom, discipline, and prudence. Solomon spends a great deal of effort developing the difference between the wise man and the foolish man, the righteous and the wicked. He gives great weight in this work to matters of choosing what is right and just and how to apply wisdom to daily life and relationships.

You know from other encounters in Scripture that seven is a special number. On the seventh day, after six consecutive days of creative labor, Genesis tells us that God rested. In John's revelation, seven letters to seven churches and seven seals tell us a great deal about God's definitive work in the future. And it isn't just the bookends of the Bible that focus on seven. The number seven appears often in Scripture and symbolizes completion.

In Proverbs 24:16, the wisdom writer doesn't mean that upon the eighth fall a righteous man can give up. The implication is that no matter how many times a righteous man falls, he will get back up.

First Corinthians 15 is about the resurrection. You may have heard the play on words associated with the word *therefore* in Scripture: Every time you see the word *therefore*, you need to ask, "What is it there for?" In this case, this last verse of chapter 15 provides the fitting response of the believer in light of the resurrection.

PROVERBS 24:16

Though a righteous man falls seven times, he will get up, but the wicked will stumble into ruin.

1 CORINTHIANS 15:58

Therefore, my dear brothers, be steadfast, immovable, always excelling in the Lord's work, knowing that your labor in the Lord is not in vain.

→ **Read Proverbs 24:16.**

Tsaddiyq is the transliterated Hebrew word for "righteous" found in Proverbs 24:16 and 65 other times in the Book of Proverbs alone.[1] It literally means just, lawful, or righteous. In that sense, it refers to the man. It is also the word used to describe the righteousness that comes from being justified by God. We know through Paul's letter to Rome that righteousness from God, apart from the law, comes through faith (Romans 3:28). We have all sinned, but through Jesus Christ we are freely justified. We are declared righteous and made righteous.

One of the marks of our new righteous character is determination. What kind of picture of determination does Proverbs 24:16 paint?

Why do you think the wicked eventually stumble into ruin? How have you seen this play out?

Do you think this is God's judgment or just how wickedness works? Explain.

→ **Read 1 Corinthians 15:58.**

What does it mean to be "steadfast" and "immovable"? Is this the same as inflexible? Why or why not?

How have you been influenced by others' attitudes of defeat?

In what ways have you seen your own attitude of defeat affect others?

The warning statement on the side mirror of our cars reads: "Objects in mirror are closer than they appear." Why is that message important? Our senses are based on perception and our senses can deceive us. Our feelings and emotions are much more closely related to our senses than to reality. God will never do His deepest work in the shallowest part of our being. People who live by feelings often live defeated lives. Your feelings will change constantly, but the truth of God remains consistent forever. If you wait until you feel like trusting and obeying, you may never get started. Faith that fails bases movement on feelings. Faith that is determined obeys regardless.

Second Corinthians 4:18 says, "We do not focus on what is seen, but on what is unseen. For what is seen is temporary, but what is unseen is eternal." What does it mean to you to persevere in spite of what you "see"?

1. "Tsaddiyq," *BibleStudyTools* [online], [cited 10 July 2012]. Available from the Internet: *www.biblestudytools.com.*

We often think of heroes in Scripture as men called by God who made an enormous impact. The calling part is right. The impact is only sometimes true. Many of God's prophets lived lives of determined faith but never achieved the result God desired. God's people often ignored and even mocked their warnings. Paul faced similar responses.

GOING DEEPER

Read Acts 14 this week. Paul traveled throughout Asia Minor on his first missionary journey. He was stoned in Iconium (v. 5) but kept preaching (v. 7). He was stoned again and run out of town in Lystra (v. 19). Yet he kept preaching.

Consider these questions and offer your response as a journal entry:

Do you readily believe what God says or do you often wait to be convinced? Why?

Do you wait until you feel like obeying God or do you step out in determined belief? Why?

What is stopping you from having a more determined faith and living according to it?

> ^{21} **After they had evangelized that town and**
> **made many disciples, they returned to Lystra,**
> **to Iconium, and to Antioch, ^{22} strengthening**
> **the disciples by encouraging them to continue**
> **in the faith and by telling them, "It is necessary**
> **to pass through many troubles on our way into**
> **the kingdom of God."** ACTS 14:21-22

Talk about determination! Paul returned to the two places where he had been stoned to continue sharing the gospel.

Memorize 1 Corinthians 15:58 and Proverbs 24:16 this week.

As a reminder to live a determined life, read the following statements aloud every day this week:

1. I am a child of God.
2. I am created in the powerful image of God.
3. God has declared me righteous.
4. My Father hears me.
5. I am filled with the Holy Spirit of God.
6. I am fully empowered by God to live a life that honors God.
7. Nothing can separate me from God's love.
8. I have died to my old way and been made alive in Christ.
9. I can obey God with joy and enthusiasm.
10. I can serve God without fear and hesitation.

PRAYER

Holy God, I commit my life to You. I am resolved to obey You completely, serve You sacrificially, and represent You well in this world. May the determination of my faith serve as an example for other believers and future generations. May You receive glory and honor and praise as a result of my life of determined faith. In the powerful name of Jesus Christ I pray. Amen.

COMPLETE
SURRENDER
DISAPPOINTMENT VS.
CONTENTMENT

READ

Do you know the story of Peter's restoration? After denying Jesus three times, Peter was brokenhearted (Matthew 26:75). Following His resurrection, Jesus appeared to His disciples, including Peter. Jesus asked Peter three times if Peter loved Him. Consider just the first instance:

> **When they had eaten breakfast, Jesus asked Simon Peter, "Simon, son of John, do you love Me more than these?"** JOHN 21:15

A great deal of attention has been given to two words in this question. The first, "love." The Greek language offers us several words for love, two of which are prominent in Scripture. *Agape* and *phileo* refer to different types of love, the first unconditional and the second brotherly. To what degree was Jesus asking if Peter loved Him? The second key word is "these." Was Jesus asking Peter if he loved his Lord more than the other disciples did? Was Jesus asking Peter if he loved his Lord more than he loved his morning catch? Did the question extend to Peter's old life and livelihood as a fisherman?

Now, imagine that you are Peter. Picture yourself being asked by Jesus if you love Him more than "these." Consider all the things you love and hold dear. Do any of them compare to the love you have for Jesus? Is it obvious to God that He alone is the supreme object of your affection? Is it true of you that no amount of disappointment or distress could deter your commitment to Christ?

That is the essence of complete surrender and total devotion.

MOVIE CLIP

View Clip 4 from the small-group DVD and then use the following discussion to start your study.

SUMMARY

Brooke Taylor longs to have children. Her husband Grant longs to give her a baby. After four years of trying, Grant learns that he is the reason for the couple's infertility. Grant and Brooke weep together after he tells her that he cannot give her children. Later he asks her if she will still love the Lord if He never gives them children. In her grief, she can't respond. Several weeks later, after feeling sick, Brooke makes an appointment with her doctor. Upon hearing from the nurse that she is still not pregnant, Brooke declares to God, through her tears, that she will still love Him.

OPEN DISCUSSION

1 What do you think it means to love God more than anything else?

2 Has it ever been difficult for you to love God when He didn't do what you wanted Him to do? Explain.

3 How do you deal with that type of disappointment?

"Life only works when Jesus is everything and we are fully submitted to Him." [1]

4 What does "Jesus is everything" mean to you?

Although true and reflective of what the Bible teaches about devotion to Christ, it can be difficult to deduce that life is "working" even when Jesus is everything and we are fully submitted. Why? Because infertility doesn't feel like life is working. Job loss doesn't feel like life is working. Childhood illness or death doesn't feel like life is working. It also doesn't feel like God is listening. The truth that everything good in life finds its proper place when God is first is difficult sometimes. However, just because a truth is difficult doesn't make it any less true.

1. "Quotes from Passion 2012," *Lawson Hembree's Blog* [online], 7 Jan. 2012 [cited 12 July 2012]. Available from the Internet: *lawsonhembree.wordpress.com*.

DISCUSS

Psalm 73 is a psalm of Asaph, the leader responsible for worship music under Davidic rule. During the days of Ezra and Nehemiah, Asaph's son would carry his legacy of musical leadership (Nehemiah 7:44). Whether these are David's words dedicated to Asaph or Asaph's words in response to his experiences in Israel is unknown.[2] In any account, the words are clear. The first portion of the psalm is a lament against the prosperity of the wicked (73:2-16). Until the psalmist steps into God's presence, his views are skewed (73:16-17). But in God's sanctuary, it all made sense. The path of the wicked, although prosperous according to the standards of the world, leads to ruin. The psalmist commits in his conclusion to trust in God and God alone. Nothing else mattered (73:25-26).

Romans 8:28-29 can be quite confusing and controversial. On one hand, verse 28 is completely abused when we adopt the belief that because we love God, everything in life will be easy and good—according to *our* measure of what is good. Far less difficult to grasp is the second part of verse 29, "to be conformed to the image of His Son."

PSALM 73:25-26

[25] Who do I have in heaven but You? And I desire nothing on earth but You. [26] My flesh and my heart may fail, but God is the strength of my heart, my portion forever.

ROMANS 8:28-29

[28] We know that all things work together for the good of those who love God: those who are called according to His purpose. [29] For those He foreknew He also predestined to be conformed to the image of His Son, so that He would be the firstborn among many brothers.

Understanding that life will not always be easy when we are completely devoted to Christ and surrendered to Him stings even more when we watch others who aren't devoted to Christ (who aren't even believers) prosper. Unbelievers are able to have children. Unbelievers get promoted. Unbelievers enjoy the same sun and rain as believers (Matthew 5:45). In those moments, in our flesh, we presume that our dedication to God doesn't pay off. This attitude is wrong. It is normal and common and human, but it is still wrong.

 Read Psalm 73:25-26.

In what (people, things, objects, identities) have you put your hope and trust? How have they failed you?

These verses speak to a desperate attitude toward God. Think of a time when you felt that same kind of desperation. Describe the need you felt for Jesus in that moment.

What does this passage reflect about a nature of constant hope in and surrender to Christ?

Even though Brooke loved God, her longing for children was becoming more important to her. God is a jealous God and guards His right to have first place in our lives. Sometimes He allows circumstances that can test our love for Him.

Why do you think God would let you experience a circumstance that tests your love for Him?

Sometimes God uses difficult or disappointing circumstances to redirect or reorient our focus if it is out of alignment with His purpose for our lives.

Describe a time when a difficulty or disappointment helped you focus more deeply on Him.

→ **Read Romans 8:28-29.**

According to this passage, what is God's purpose for us?

God's ultimate desire, His proclamation of what is good, is that you would be more like Jesus. According to verse 28, *all* things—good, bad, ugly, disappointing, difficult, confusing, hurtful, trying, painful, joyful, easy, fun, necessary, surprising, miraculous, forgettable, regretful, harmful, tearful—can be used for good. And what is that good? That you would become more like Jesus.

How does that understanding of God's purpose shape your understanding of your difficult circumstances?

2. "Psalm 73:1," *BibleStudyTools* [online], [cited 10 July 2012]. Available from the Internet: *www.biblestudytools.com*.

The first time the word *love* appears in Scripture speaks of Abraham's love for his son Isaac. The only child of Abraham and his wife Sarah, Isaac was a walking miracle. Isaac was given to the couple although they were well beyond childbearing years (Hebrews 11:11-12). Isaac was the seed through whom God's promise to Abraham would be fulfilled. Many generations would come to call Isaac their great ancestor. Abraham loved his son. So God decided to test Abraham's faith and commitment.

GOING DEEPER

Read Genesis 22:1-14. What is most significant about the sacrifice God requested?

What is your "Isaac"? What do you dearly love that would be nearly unthinkable for you to give up?

Is your love for your Isaac more important to you than your love for God?

This story is known by Christians to be an Old Testament picture of Jesus Christ. One day God would offer the sacrifice He requested of Abraham when He gave Jesus. Abraham even said in verse 8 that God Himself would provide the lamb for the altar. Just as Isaac carried the wood for the fire, Jesus carried the wood of the cross. Just as Isaac obeyed his father and placed himself on the altar, Jesus obeyed His Father and willingly laid down His life. Jesus was the lamb of whom Abraham spoke. It is God's love for Jesus and gift of Jesus that helps us understand God's great love for us.

- Your joy in the midst of trials reflects your love for God over your own comfort and pleasure.
- Your gratitude for difficulty reflects your understanding of God's greater purpose for your life.
- Your commitment to God during pain reflects your declaration that God is your portion no matter what happens.

Memorize Psalm 73:25-26 this week.

Make this passage your motto when times are good and especially when they aren't.

PRAYER

Make a list of things for which you are grateful. Include ways you recognize God working and responding to your prayers. Gratitude is the cure for disappointment.

The path to contentment is paved with surrender. As you close this study, pray that God will continue to help you face your giants with confidence and determination. Pray that He will help you live your life in complete submission to Him. Recognizing God's authority is music to God's ears. Give Him praise with your words of commitment and your life of submission.

APPENDIX 1
When Life Is Tough

Grant Taylor entered in to what some might call the perfect storm of troubles. He had issues personally and professionally. He hadn't won a season of football since he began as head coach of the Shiloh Eagles. He had parents, faculty, and even his assistant coach questioning his ability. His car was on its last leg and his house stunk, literally. To top it off, after four years of trying, he hadn't been able to give his wife the one thing she desired most, a child. The discovery that his job was in jeopardy and that he was the reason for the couple's infertility was the final straw.

Grant made the wise choice. He went to God's Word. He found strength on his knees and in God's vision for his life and ultimate purpose for the team. He put his family in God's hands and trusted his heavenly Father for provision. But, unfortunately, we aren't guaranteed an out just because we pray. And we can't be certain that our problems will go away just because we commit ourselves to honoring God.

You may be facing your own storm of problems. You may need additional help to process and heal from the circumstances you are dealing with. Know that there is no shame in seeking that help. Just like Grant and Brooke, the strongest thing you can do is to admit your weakness to God and your need for help.

God's grace is greater than our sin. His power is greater than our problems. But some problems require more help. If you are the victim of abuse, you need to report the abuse and seek counseling to help you heal. If you are suffering from depression, there is no weakness in seeking help. Seek out the counsel of your pastor. Be open to any referral he might make. There are people and tools available to you that God can use to work powerfully in your life.

Engaging in a study like this is a great first step. For some, it may be all you need to reorient your life toward God and His Word and the healing process you need. For others, additional work will be required. But if you are willing to admit your pain and accept help, your reward will be great.

Leader Notes

Prepare for an exciting adventure as you facilitate the *Facing the Giants* small-group study! Available resources include this member book and a DVD leader kit (item 005533951). Movie clips and a movie trailer are on the Bible study DVD in the kit.

Read through the entire member book and then go back and prepare for each session with your group in mind. Make notes and go deep into the Scriptures. Consider ways to involve members. Most groups meet for an hour, but you can expand the schedule if time and location allow. Be sure to include prayer. These are the suggested time frames:

10 minutes	Opening comments and Read
15 minutes	Watch
20 minutes	Discuss
15 minutes	Live and closure

For group sessions 2-4, give members an opportunity to briefly share insights from what the Lord has shown them over the past week. Include this as a part of your opening time.

Clip themes and lengths:
Clip 1: Wholehearted (6:32)
Clip 2: Attempt the Impossible (1:25)
Clip 3: Never Give Up (1:25)
Clip 4: Complete Surrender (5:06)

APPENDIX 3
Study Options

Perhaps you are going through this study as part of your Sunday School class or weekly small group. Have you considered the value of sharing the things you are learning with others? Here are four ways you might take this study and use it as a model of discipleship with others in your life.

A Family Affair

Facing the Giants is a PG film, making it appropriate for older children and teens. Schedule a family movie night and watch the film. Pop some corn; make ice cream sundaes; rearrange furniture so everyone has the best seat in the house; put on your pajamas; turn out the lights; enjoy the movie.

After the movie, ask your kids if they would like to spend one night a week for the next four weeks doing a family Bible study together.

Here are some kid-friendly questions and family Bible study tips to use for each session.

Session 1: Wholehearted
1. Are there times when you don't feel like doing your best?
2. What can we (parents/family) do to help you do your best in school? Sports? Other activities?
3. Do you think it's important to do your best with your home responsibilities? Why?
4. Why do you think Paul was still writing letters to churches from prison?
5. What things can we do better as a family in order to honor God more?

Tip: Have kids take turns reading the passages of Scripture and the sections of the study guide.
Tip: Set up a reward system for Scripture memory. This shouldn't be considered a bribe, but an incentive to take Scripture memory seriously. Even if a child's motive for learning God's Word starts with reward, the benefit is immeasurable.

Session 2: Attempt the Impossible

1. What impossible thing do you dream of doing one day?
2. What impossible things can we try as a family in order to serve God?
3. The account of Jesus feeding the 5,000 in John 6:5-13 includes the specific detail of the little boy who brought the five loaves and two fish. The boy and his lunch were used by Jesus to do a miracle that day. Do you believe God can do impossible things in your life even though you are young? Why or why not?

Tip: Consider family missions. Schedule a Saturday of service where you explore opportunities to help others and volunteer with local service agencies. Make sure you check the organizations' age policies before attending with your kids. Build up to a short-term family mission trip where the entire family goes to serve somewhere else, maybe even internationally.

Session 3: Never Give Up

1. Have you ever felt like quitting something? What was it? Why did you feel that way?
2. Why is it important to keep trying until we succeed?
3. Is there something new that you would like to try but are nervous about failing?
4. What does the word *determined* mean to you?
5. How can we be a family who is more determined to live for God?

Tip: Create a family goals chart that lists goals and action steps for each family member. Celebrate family members as they reach their goals.

Session 4: Complete Surrender

1. Why do you think Peter denied Jesus after Jesus was arrested?
2. How do you show God that you love Him?
3. What difficult situations have you been through and learned from? What lessons did you learn?
4. Do you think learning something important and getting closer to God make difficulty worth it in the end? Why or why not?
5. What do you think God might want you to give up in order to love Him more?
6. What things might we need to change or give up as a family in order to show God more love?

Tip: Share God's plan of salvation with your kids if they haven't made a decision to trust Jesus for salvation yet. If your child is ready and understands what it means to make his or her own decision to follow Christ, check out the following resources from LifeWay (*www.lifeway.com*).

I'm a Christian Now! Younger Kids (Item 005191565)
I'm a Christian Now! Older Kids (Item 005191566)
I'm a Christian, Now What? (Item 005490151)

Follow up with your pastor or age-graded minister at your church so that he or she can help you take the next steps.

A Neighborhood Gathering

Consider doing the *Facing the Giants* study as a neighborhood gathering. Start with a movie night by inviting neighbors to your home to view the film. Invite others to join you on a consistent day and time for the next month to engage the study together. This is a great "front door" activity to your church. A front door is any point of contact that an unchurched person has with a local group of believers. Being part of your casual home Bible study may be just what they need in order to connect to Christ and church before they are willing to attend a Sunday service. As you do this study with unbelievers, be prepared to do the following:

- Provide Bibles for those who do not have one of their own.
- Help unchurched people find passages of Scripture.
- Explain your testimony and why you have chosen to trust Christ for salvation.
- Present the gospel.

Make this gathering a family affair by including kids if the people you invite have children. Consider doing a potluck dinner each week, ordering pizza, or at least having drinks and dessert. Food enhances fellowship. Stronger fellowship enhances small-group Bible study.

An Office Small Group

Invite a group of coworkers to join you for a few weeks early in the morning, over lunch, or after work hours to participate in this study. This is a great way to get to know your coworkers better and to establish your faith in the workplace. (Note: It is probably best to stick with a same-sex group to avoid any potential issues for you as the group leader.)

WARNING: As you lead this study and become more open about your faith, two things can and probably will happen.

1. People may begin to depend on you and seek you out for counsel. You will naturally become someone they are comfortable sharing intimate parts of life with because you have established yourself as someone who will listen and pray and offer godly advice. To be helpful and not harmful, you will need to stay strong in God's Word. You can't share His truth if you don't know what it says. You will need to be consistent in your prayer life so that the Holy Spirit's power will be evident in you. You will need to rely on the Holy Spirit for wisdom and power in order to help others.

2. People will begin to watch you closely. Unbelievers can be highly suspicious of people who claim to be Christians. They may have been hurt by an inconsistent believer before and are on guard for you to do the same. Don't be put off or offended. Their judgment of you is out of pain or fear. People who are antagonistic to faith need regular demonstration of who Christ is before they can come to trust and believe. You will need to walk consistently with Christ in order to prove who He is and who you are because of Him. How you live, work, and interact with others are things they will be looking for. Unbelievers will want to know if who you are in Christ is real or fake. Rely on Christ's power and your own prayer life to walk worthy of Jesus in your workplace.

Small-Group Quick Tips

1. Distribute the responsibility.

As a leader, the temptation is always to do everything personally; that quickly leads to frustration. Your main focus is to prepare the lesson in advance and prioritize the most important aspects during class discussion. Divvy maintenance tasks such as keeping track of attendance, prayer request follow-up, and refreshment sign-ups. In group meetings, ask different members to read Scripture and sections of content and to lead out in discussion.

2. Make the group a safe place.

Remind your group weekly as you engage in open discussion about the sensitivity of things people may share. Keep confidentiality and respect in focus.

3. Set the pace.

As a leader, you set the pace for your group. Your willingness to share and be transparent will have a direct impact on others' willingness to do the same. Your advance preparation and commitment to start and end on time will influence the group's direction. Your desire to stay on task and not chase rabbits will indicate what is appropriate and inappropriate in terms of group dynamics.

4. Be comfortable with silent moments and unanswered questions.

Often silence creates discomfort for a leader who may feel pressure to fill the awkwardness by talking more. As a leader, be OK with long pauses. Sometimes this is just an indication that the question has warranted more thought.

Some people may present difficult life challenges. Often they aren't looking for answers as much as a listening ear. Be sensitive but guide conversations to stay focused. Sometimes you may only recognize the difficulty of the situation and acknowledge the need to seek the Lord when answers are not clear.

5. Pray for your group members.

Oswald Chambers has said, "Prayer does not equip us for greater works—prayer is the greater work."[1] How you commit to praying for your group is much more valuable than how well you lead your group. In fact, how well you lead will be a direct reflection of how well you pray for the people in your group.

Commit to pray for the people God has entrusted to you, that they will:
- have eyes that are open to see God move
- have ears that hear the Word and commit to doing what it says
- genuinely repent of sin as the Holy Spirit convicts them through God's Word
- grow spiritually and begin to develop a daily intimate walk with the Lord
- make wise choices
- be committed to the group study
- live lives of integrity in their homes, communities, and places of work
- lead their children well
- be committed to their spouses
- trust Christ in any and all circumstances of life
- be free from temptation and the attacks of the Enemy
- take on the full armor of God as both their defense and offense in the spiritual battles they face
- love God supremely and love others well

1. "The Key of the Greater Work," *My Utmost for His Highest* [online] 17 Oct. 2012 [cited 14 July 2012]. Available on the Internet: *http://utmost.org*.

Icebreakers

Starting your group time each week can be done in a number of ways. Use any of the icebreakers or suggestions provided here or develop a plan that works for the dynamic of your group.

Hot Seat

If your group is small enough (no more than eight members), you may choose to do a weekly "hot seat." Sign each member up for a week to be the object of your group's attention for the initial few minutes. Direct each member to the following questions before your study starts so he or she will be prepared when it is time to share. In the hot seat, the member will answer as quickly as possible each of the following questions designed to help you get to know one another in a fun way.

1. What was your favorite childhood memory?
2. Describe your high school self in three words.
3. What brought you to (this town) and (this church)?
4. What is the best thing about life right now?
5. How can the group pray for you specifically?

Conclude each hot seat session by surrounding the group member and praying for him or her. You may do the hot seat activity for up to two members per week. Beyond that, it begins to take up more time than it needs to.

Fact or Fiction

Ask each group member to write three things on an index card, two items that are true about them and one item that is complete fiction. Collect and shuffle the cards. One by one, the leader will read the cards aloud. Group members guess who wrote the card and then which of the three items is false. This is a fun, non-threatening way to build community and get to know one another.

Constant Questions

Form a circle in your group. You may stand or sit. Start with the leader and move clockwise around the circle asking the person to your left a question. The catch is that no question is ever answered. A person is eliminated if they repeat a question that has already been asked, hesitate and can't come up with a new question quickly enough, or forget the rule and begin to answer the question they were asked. As you play, members will be eliminated one by one. At the end, two members will remain for the final battle.

Deserted Island

Tell the group that they have been exiled to a deserted island. Share with them that in addition to their spouse and essential items they may also take one book other than the Bible, one piece of music, and one luxury item. Allow time for everyone to share what they would bring.

Would You Rather

Divide your group into teams of no more than four people each. Give each team a sheet of paper and have them write a list of fun, humorous, or thought provoking "would you rather" questions. Take turns having each group ask one question at a time and allowing everyone to vote by raising their hand.

Here are a few examples:
1. Would you rather only eat your favorite food and nothing else for the rest of your life or be able to eat anything else except that one item?
2. Would you rather have a root canal or mole removal?
3. Would you rather vacation in the mountains or on the beach?

Follow-Up Resources

- *The Ways of God: How God Reveals Himself Before a Watching World*
  (item 005500139)
- *Faith Limps: Trusting a Good God in a Broken World*
  (member, item 005471380; leader kit, item 005471379)
- *Presence: Overwhelmed by God*
  (member, item 005371605; leader kit, item 005371604)
- *Fresh: Reviving Stale Faith*
  (member, item 005470700; leader kit, item 005470699)
- *Stolen* (member, item 005469706; leader kit, item 005469705)
- *Always True: God's Promises When Life Is Hard*
  (member, item 005371573; leader kit, item 005274675)
- *When Life Is Hard: Turning Your Trials to Gold*
  (member, item 005293072; leader kit, item 005271225)
- *Outlive Your Life* (member, item 005271299; leader kit, item 005189411)
- *Crave: An Exploration of the Human Spirit*
  (member, item 005271313; leader kit, item 005271665)
- *Gospel Revolution: Recovering the Power of Christianity*
  (member, item 005467769; leader kit, item 005467771)
- *Honor Begins at Home: The COURAGEOUS Bible Study*
  (member, item 005371686; leader kit, item 005325609)
- *Courageous Living Bible Study*
  (member, item 005422891; leader kit, item 005371695)
- *The Love Dare Bible Study*
  (member, item 005186345; leader kit, item 005179026)
- *Unconditional: The Bible Study*
  (member, item 005490148; leader kit, item 005490147)

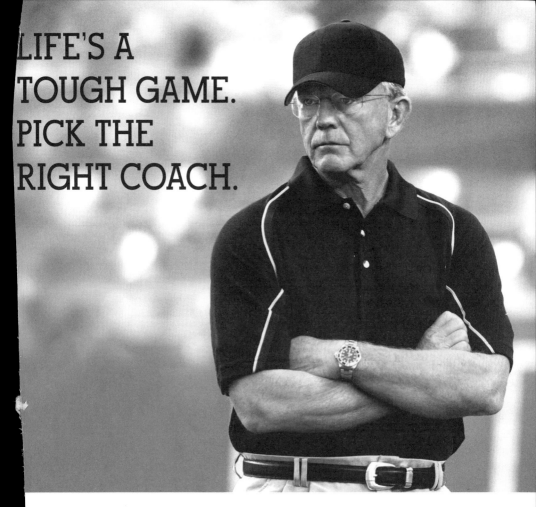

LIFE'S A TOUGH GAME. PICK THE RIGHT COACH.

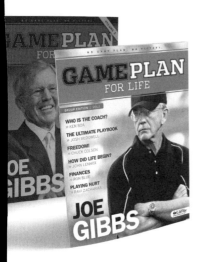

Joe Gibbs has won the Super Bowl three times without taking a single hit. He's raced to three NASCAR championships but never left pit row. How did he do it? By finding quality people who could make it happen for him. And now he's doing the same for you. Today's man is struggling with tough issues, like sex, money, health, and salvation. Joe tackles these and other topics in his *Game Plan for Life* studies, with insightful assistance from handpicked experts like Chuck Colson, Ravi Zacharias, Josh McDowell, Tony Evans, and more. It's a virtual dream team that can help you create an ideal game plan for your life. Visit us online for more information and free samples.

LifeWay | Men

IT ALL BEGINS WITH A STORY.

A good story has the power to move people like nothing else. LifeWay Films harness the power of story to share the gospel of Jesus Christ. With Licenses starting at just $49, a movie is a perfect, cost-effective tool for your next community outreach or church-wide event.

TO LEARN MORE, CALL 1.800.458.2772

OR VISIT LIFEWAY.COM/FILMS

LifeWay | Films
MOVING PICTURES